Beware of the Frog

by Isabel Thomas

Lean, Mean ... and Green

You might not think of frogs as fearsome creatures. However, they are not always quiet and cautious.

Some frogs are loud and bright. Some frogs are **toxic**. These features help frogs scare **predators**. They even helped frogs outlast the T. rex!

Ready to Pop

Frogs and toads are snack-sized for many predators. However, they have tricks to avoid being caught. Some give enemies the impression they are BIGGER than they really are.

This Mexican burrowing toad feels threatened. It takes a big gulp of air to stretch its skin. Its body inflates like a balloon!

Shocking Screams

Some frogs make loud noises to cause confusion. This frog is known as the 'screaming toad'. When annoyed, it lets out a high-pitched scream.

It sounds just like an angry cat! Then it traps and bites its victim.

The screaming toad also has fangs!

Not So Scrumptious

A layer of **mucus** stops a frog's skin drying out. This slime often contains atrocious **toxins**. This frog is not a tasty snack!

What if a predator catches a toxic frog? It is taught to spit the frog out. It must not swallow it!

This is the golden poison dart frog. It is one of the most toxic animals on Earth. Its skin is so toxic, it could kill two elephants!

However, a frog wants to avoid being eaten at all! This is why poison dart frogs have bright patches of skin. It tells predators to be suspicious.

Can you see why this is called a strawberry poison dart frog?

Red Alert

In the wild, red is often a sign of danger. A tomato frog is no exception! If attacked, its skin releases an explosion of sticky mucus. This **irritates** a predator's mouth.

Tree frogs can alarm predators with a simple stare!

Dressed to Kill

Congolese giant toads have a special dressing-up trick. It is an artificial snake costume! Their shape and patterns match those of a deadly snake.

This causes confusion among predators. They don't want to risk a mistake! They avoid both animals.

Maximum Aggression

The hairy frog has an extreme reaction to predators. If attacked, it breaks its own toe bones. It makes claws!

The splinters of bone poke out of the frog's skin. They can scratch anything that gets too close.

Male African giant bullfrogs protect their **clutch** of eggs. If they are threatened, they are not calm. They will leap to attack any invasion of their space.

The bullfrogs have no **qualms** about attacking potential predators. They even have sharp teeth hidden in their lower jaw.

Playing Dead

Some frogs are like magicians. They have a naughty trick up their sleeves.

They freeze. Then they flop onto their backs. Finally, they display their bellies and play dead!

The bright belly tells predators they are dangerous!

This frog has a clever way to avoid suspicion. Its skin looks like moss. When threatened, it curls up on a mossy bank and plays dead.

Finding the frog is almost an impossible mission!

Glossary

clutch: a group of eggs laid at the same time

irritates: hurts, bothers or annoys

mucus: sticky or slimy stuff made by an animal

predators: animals that hunt and eat other animals

qualms: feelings of worry

toxic: poisonous

toxins: harmful poisons or venoms

Index